IMPRESSIVE DRILLING RIGS

BY NATALIE HUMPHREY

Gareth Stevens
PUBLISHING

Please visit our website, www.garethstevens.com. For a free color catalog of all our high-quality books, call toll free 1-800-542-2595 or fax 1-877-542-2596.

Portions of this work were originally authored by Kenny Allen and published as *Drilling Rigs*. All new materials in I this edition authored by Natalie Humphrey.

Cataloging-in-Publication Data

Names: Humphrey, Natalie.
Title: Impressive drilling rigs / Natalie Humphrey.
Description: New York : Gareth Stevens Publishing, 2023. | Series: Mega machines! | Includes glossary and index.
Identifiers: ISBN 9781538283073 (pbk.) | ISBN 9781538283097 (library bound) | ISBN 9781538283103 (ebook)
Subjects: LCSH: Oil well drilling rigs–Juvenile literature.
Classification: LCC TN871.5 H86 2023 | DDC 622'.33810284–dc23

Published in 2023 by
Gareth Stevens Publishing
2455 Clinton Street
Buffalo, NY 14224

Copyright © 2023 Gareth Stevens Publishing

Designer: Deanna Paternostro
Editor: Natalie Humphrey

Photo credits: Cover, p. 1 Eddytb Foto/Shutterstock.com; pp. 3, 4, 6, 8, 10, 12, 14, 16, 18, 20, 21 (bottom), 22, 23, 24 Nataliia K/Shutterstock.com; p. 5 Pattadon Ajarasingh/Shutterstock.com; p. 7 phetsamay philavanh/Shutterstock.com; p. 9 Evgeny_V/Shutterstock.com; pp. 11, 13 James Jones Jr/Shutterstock.com; p. 15 I am a Stranger/Shutterstock.com; p. 17 zhuda/Shutterstock.com; p. 19 Aussie Family Living/Shutterstock.com; p. 21 (top) Henrik Lehnerer.

Printed in the United States of America

Some of the images in this book illustrate individuals who are models. The depictions do not imply actual situations or events.

CPSIA compliance information: Batch #CW23GS: For further information contact Gareth Stevens at 1-800-542-2595.

Find us on

CONTENTS

Boldface words appear in the glossary.

Mega Drilling Rigs

Drilling rigs are mega machines that dig giant holes in the ground. Only one person is needed to run the smallest drilling rigs. Hundreds of workers are needed to run the biggest drilling rigs. These rigs can be bigger than a house!

Prepare for Drilling!

Building a drilling rig is hard work. First, the workers prepare the land that the drilling rig will go on. They cut down trees, build roads for the trucks, and dig pads where the drilling rig will go. Sometimes they dig a pit for **waste** rock.

Powering the Rig

Drilling rigs use many different kinds of power to do their work. Some use gas **engines** like those used in cars. Others run on **electricity**. The power source is set up when workers prepare the land for drilling.

Building the Rig

After the land is ready and the power is set up, it's time to build the drilling rig! First, workers set up the derrick. A derrick is a tall metal **frame** that holds the drill in place. It has ropes or cables that raise and lower the drill.

Drill Bits

Drill bits are strong tools at the end of drills. The drill bit cuts through dirt and rock as the drill pipe goes into the ground. Some bits spin. Some bits have blades that cut rock. Some pound rock like a hammer.

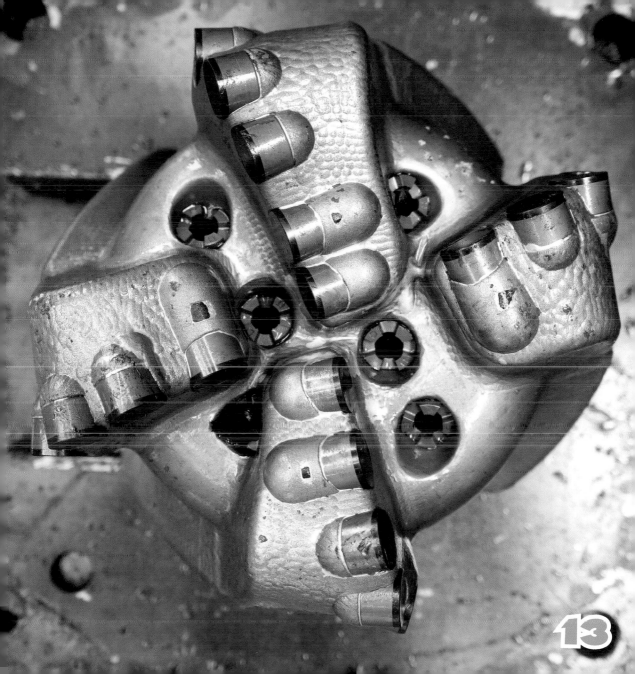

The Borehole

A borehole is the hole made in the ground by the drilling rig. The derrick lowers the drill to make the borehole. Boreholes are needed to reach water to make wells. Boreholes are used to reach oil and natural gas too.

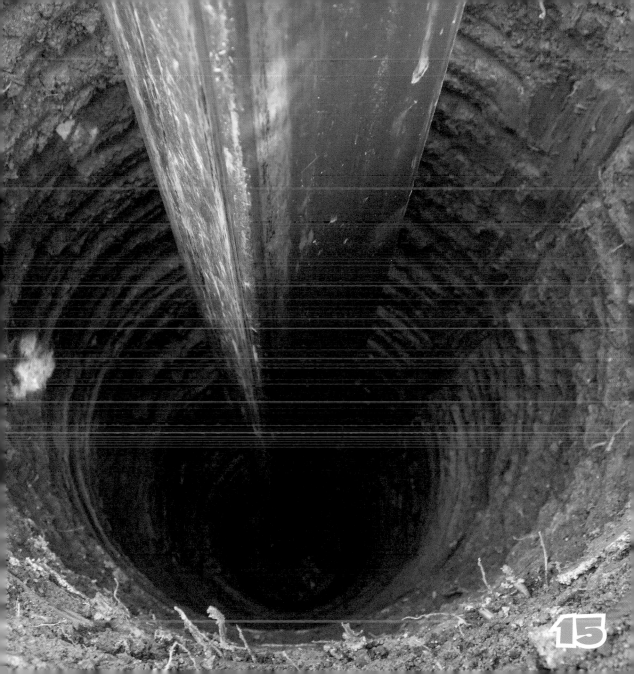

Drilling Deep

After the borehole is made, workers put a drill string down the hole. A drill string is made of thick, steel pipe that **connects** the drill bit to the surface. When drilling starts, the drill string turns and digs deeper into the ground.

Dirty Work

As the drill rig works, mud is pushed up the borehole. The mud forces dirt and waste rock to the top of the borehole where it is removed. Workers place the dirt and rocks in different pits.

Bigger Than Big

Some of the biggest drilling rigs are built in the ocean! These drilling rigs are used to drill oil out of the ocean floor. Some of these rigs are built on **platforms** and can be big enough for people to live on!

Mega Machine Facts: Hibernia Drilling Rig

Location: Newfoundland, Canada

Weight: 639,340 tons (580,000 mt)

Number of Drills: 64

Barrels of oil drilled: 126,000 barrels a day

Drill Depth: 12,139 feet (3,700 m) below sea level

GLOSSARY

connect: To join together.

depth: How deep something is below the surface.

electricity: A type of energy that powers machines and flows through cables.

engine: A machine that makes power.

frame: Something that holds up or gives shape to something else.

platform: A flat surface that is higher than another surface, including a structure with legs that supports a rig that drills for oil at sea.

waste: Material that is left over and unwanted after something is built or a project is completed.

FOR MORE INFORMATION

BOOKS

Holdren, Annie C. *Building An Offshore Oil Rig*. Mankato, MN: Amicus/Amicus Ink, 2020.

Rogers, Marie. *Gigantic Drilling Rigs*. New York, NY: PowerKids Press, 2022.

WEBSITES

Britannica Kids: Rotary Drilling Rig
kids.britannica.com/students/assembly/view/130180
Learn about the different parts of a drilling rig.

Energy Education
energyeducation.ca/encyclopedia/Oil_well
Learn about different types of wells drilled by drilling rigs.

INDEX